Sharps Cabaret

As impressive as the distance in space Katy Giebenhain's beautiful poems travel—from the Appalachian Trail to Germany—is the depth of the human experience they explore. Here, offered up with a lyrical voice and (often) with wry humor, is Giebenhain's world, which, because she invokes it so well, becomes our world.

—Mark Brazaitis, author of *The Other Language: Poems* and *The Incurables: Stories*

One after the other, the poems in *Sharps Cabaret* are engaging, concise, and precisely observed. It was a pleasure to read this book.

—Gary Fincke, author of *Bringing Back the Bones: New and Selected Poems*

Vibrant, deep, witty, and thought-provoking, *Sharps Cabaret* takes on questions of identity, history, language, religion, and living with a chronic illness. Giebenhain's poems are at once supple and tough, and always surprising.

—George Ella Lyon, author of *Many-Storied House*, Kentucky Poet Laureate 2015–2016

These are poems that come from long looking, persistent questioning, and honest wondering. Amid the gritty details of ordinary life, they sing with musicality, wit, and poetic intelligence.

—Mark Burrows, professor of Religion and Literature at the University of Applied Sciences, Bochum (Germany), and author of two recent volumes of poetry in translation: Rainer Maria Rilke, *Prayers of a Young Poet* and SAID, *99 Psalms*

MERCER UNIVERSITY PRESS

Endowed by

TOM WATSON BROWN

and

THE WATSON-BROWN FOUNDATION, INC.

Sharps Cabaret

Poems

Katy Giebenhain

MERCER UNIVERSITY PRESS | *Macon, Georgia*
2017

MUP/ P543

© 2017 by Mercer University Press
Published by Mercer University Press
1501 Mercer University Drive
Macon, Georgia 31207

9 8 7 6 5 4 3 2 1

Books published by Mercer University Press are printed on acid-free paper
that meets the requirements of the American National Standard for
Information Sciences—Permanence of Paper for Printed Library Materials.

ISBN   978-0-88146-641-0
Cataloging-in-Publication Data is available from the Library of Congress

Winner of the Adrienne Bond Poetry Award

PREVIOUS WINNERS

Seaborn Jones, *Going Farther into the Woods than the Woods Go*
(published 2012)

Kelly Whiddon, *The House Began to Pitch*
(published 2013)

Megan Sexton, *Swift Hour*
(published 2014)

Philip Lee Williams, *The Color of All Things: 99 Love Poems*
(published 2015)

Lesley Dauer, *Carnival Life*
(published 2016)

ACKNOWLEDGMENTS

Thank you to the editors who first published these poems in journals or anthologies. "Glucose Self-Monitoring" and "The Accidental German" first appeared in *Prairie Schooner*. "1969" first appeared in *Water~Stone Review*. "Replica" and "To a Hanover Potato Chip" first appeared in *The Hanover Evening Sun*. "Forget Beauty" and "Miss Hydraulic Fracturing" first appeared in *Appalachian Journal*. "Obelisks" first appeared in *Die unsterblichen Obelisken Ägyptens*. "Song for Type 1 Diabetes" first appeared in *Motif I: Writing by Ear*. "Pretending to be Italian" appeared in *The Emancipator* and received the George Scarbrough Prize for Poetry. "The Boxer's Dog" and "James Bond and the Type 1 Diabetic Bridesmaid" first appeared in *The Lumière Reader*. "I am Ready to go Home" first appeared in *The London Magazine*. "Abraham Lincoln's Pontiac" first appeared in *Hidden City Quarterly*. "The Gatekeepers" first appeared in the chapbook *Absent Photographer*. "Foreign Language for Adults" first appeared in the chapbook *Pretending to be Italian*. "Lord, in Your Mercedes, Hear our Prayer" first appeared in *The Cresset*. "Flying Low Over Chester County, Pennsylvania at Night," "First Day of the Battle" and "Red Baron Singles" first appeared in *Backbone Mountain Review*. "Girl-Moses" first appeared in *Tokens for the Foundlings*. "Little Prophets" and "Green Card Prayer on the Turnpike" first appeared in *Vineyards: A Journal of Christian Poetry*. "Reisekapellen" first appeared in *Spiritus: A Journal of Christian Spirituality*. "Christmas Eve, Feeding the Bull Calves" first appeared in *Saint Katherine Review*. "Itasca" first appeared in *Down to the Dark River: Poems about the Mississippi River*. "Robin Hood is Gone" first appeared on the blog *Better Living through Beowulf*. "Falling Asleep in a 300 Year-Old Industrial Cottage in Derbyshire Surrounded by Star Wars Action Figures," "Marlboro Country" and "Hunting Season" first appeared in *Glasgow Review of Books*. "Kitchen Meditation on the 22nd Article of the Augsburg Confession" first appeared in *Bearings Online*. "Suddenly I Love my Hair" first appeared in *The Healing Muse*. "Recalibrating the CGM on a Bench in Kensington Gardens" first appeared in *The Examined Life Journal*.

The epigraph to "Another Ex-Expatriate" is from *Ahead of All Parting: The Selected Poetry and Prose of Rainer Maria Rilke* edited and translated by Stephen Mitchell (New York: The Modern Library, 1995). "Lord, in Your Mercedes, Hear our Prayer" refers to a line in the "Light Side" rubric from the February, 2007 issue of *The Lutheran* magazine. "Farm Road" is the title of an Andrew Wyeth painting and a line from this poem is from John Wilmerding's *Andrew

Wyeth: The Helga Pictures (New York: Harry N. Abrams, Inc., 1978). The epigraph to "Forget Beauty" is from *Copperhead Cane* by Jim Wayne Miller (Louisville KY: Green River Writers/Grex Press, 1995). "First Day of the Battle" is after *The Colors of Courage: Gettysburg's Forgotten History: Immigrants, Women, and African Americans in the Civil War's Defining Battle* by Margaret Creighton (New York: Basic Books, 2005)

Special thanks go to the staff at Mercer University Press, to Peter Kuhn, to impresarios Gary Ciocco and Marty Malone, to Tony Curtis at University of South Wales, to John Spangler and Maria Erling at Gettysburg Seminary, to Kendra Kopelke at University of Baltimore, to the Hanover crit. group, to Amanda Graham, The Collegeville Institute, Gladstone's Library, The Glen West Workshop, The Mountain Heritage Literary Festival, to the brilliant Holbrook-writing-divas and to Ron and Candy Giebenhain.

CONTENTS

III.

IV.

For Dan Lund and Susan Fuhr, in memory

Sharps Cabaret

I. Pitching Horseshoes in Saigon

Forget Beauty

For translators, who carry meaning across frontiers
to other cultures and countries.
— Jim Wayne Miller

Forget family, inheritance,
the name
of any mountain, holler,
creek, county, neighbor you know.
But especially, forget beauty.

Because they're deaf
to your beauty.
Make it *their* water, *their* anger
their lungs, *their* ticking clocks,
their children's children.
Preach past the choir.
Turn the truth. Plough it,
catch it, thread it, hand-carry it
from one world to another.

Sky-write their horizon with facts.
Occupy them with facts.
Open-mouth-kiss-them with facts,
with battlefield improvisation,
with missionary zeal.
You know both languages.
Do it right. They'll never know
what hit them.

Foreign Language for Adults

Once talk came easily as breath,
high-chair bound,
massaging the tray
with a chicken leg,
flinging sounds
around the dining room.

But this is sink or swim.
This is learning and knowing
that it's learning.
It can be picked up, I'm told.
Like dry cleaning?
Like a few pounds?
Like men in a Fells Point bar?
Picked up in no time.
But it's been some time since
my tongue's indenture.

Remember Girl Scout singing?
Make new friends
but keep the old
one is silver
and the other gold.
I step and sing and breathe
with my new friend,
my silver throat.

Abraham Lincoln's Pontiac

After seeing that kiss
behind the 1st Massachusetts Memorial,
Boy Scouts storm the spine of the lookout tower.
Below them, Toyotas haul
their air conditioned hulls around the battlefield.
Reenactors already stopped shaving.
The bone and wool layer of that summer
settles deeper into the earth.

Lee and Longstreet speak in acrylic
below the post office clock.
Meade broods from a hospital hallway. No accident,
the beard behind this windshield
as Abraham Lincoln's Pontiac
pulls into the alley off Hay Street
(the Elvis of Gettysburg).

I am the horse turning left
past walls of brick, sharpshooter-stung.
At the stoplight, Harley riders
place heels on the pavement.
I jiggle my mane for the heck of it.
A hoop-skirted woman winks
at me while talking into her mobile phone.
There are no lukewarm enthusiasts here,
only HUGE fans, experts, buffs.
Do you have a link?
I do. She pulled a gun for Chamberlain,
that summer, as I pull tourists now.

Glucose Self-Monitoring

A stabbing in miniature, it is,
a tiny crime,
my own blood parceled
drop by drop and set
on the flickering tongue
of this machine.

It is the spout-punching of trees
for syrup new and smooth
and sweeter
than nature ever intended.
It is Sleeping Beauty's curse
and fascination.
It is the dipstick measuring of oil
from the Buick's throat,
the necessary maintenance.

It is every vampire movie ever made.

Hand, my martyr without lips,
my quiet cow.
I'll milk your fingertips
for all they're worth.
For what they're worth.

Something like a harvest, it is,
a tiny crime.

Hunting Season

County roads churn with hooves
and haunches.
Deer throw themselves at cars
like sailors dizzy
from Lorelei song
as if these boulders lined
the river Rhine
and the siren trilled magic
from a bank barn.

This deer, tonight's near-miss,
buffs the driver's side
of a Subaru before springing
into the trees.
It's an instant. A touching but
not-quite-meeting:
the sweep of a stranger's knuckles
in the subway,
a shark's shadow lanning the water,
too close, or the invisible fence
in a blizzard,
catching a lost body, saving
by a shoulder's brush, tickle, grazing.

How startling it is when space
is not wholly yours
the way you thought it was.

Falling Asleep in a 300-Year-Old Industrial Cottage in Derbyshire Surrounded by Star Wars Action Figures

Did you know a Storm Trooper Red Eye
has higher mechanical skills
than battle skills?

Did you know an Imperial Storm Trooper
has higher leadership skills
than intelligence?

Flanked by shelves of Jedi
a weekend houseguest
channels Joseph Campbell, says

out loud, in the snug dark
What about the Non-Hero's journey?
Alongside the call to adventure
are the other calls.
And someone appears at the right time:
the enemy with a thousand faces
the mentor with a thousand faces
the waitress with a thousand faces.
The Hero doesn't get
through anything alone.
All creators worth their salt know this.

1969

I. Soldier with Typewriter

At a certain speed
keystrokes land like hooves
on blue clay,
chopping firewood with more
than one axe swinging,
Howie the barber's shears in action.
At a certain speed they sound
like helicopter blades.
The air is thick with them.

And the kid the newbies pegged
for infantry, the tall one
with glasses and small hands
for being such a goddamned
good basketball player,
could type. And a certain speed
was needed just then.
Surprising himself,
he'd ammunition in his knuckles,
in the quarter-turning
of his neck, back and forth
above the pert Lettera 32.

At his desk the jungle whispered,
chided through plywood
to his sunburned ears.

A certain speed kept her quiet.

II. Pitching Horseshoes in Saigon

Through skies he didn't even need
a passport to enter, he brought shoes,
decided beforehand
this tour would be a glass half-full,
yanked stakes from familiar ground,
rammed them into place,
(much deeper in sand—much).

Free time was never so expensive.
Right arm posed, home held
in each crouch unwinding, he kept it up,
taught others the follow-through arcs
until many ears strained
for the *tchingk* of a ringer.

Here was symmetry—the long
arm of the farm—distance controlled,
straw bales or duffel bags,
broken fences or charts
for his commander, games changed,
but work was work,
and free time was never so expensive.
Marking each block of day,
he went on as he'd begun,
the weight
and shape
of luck in his hands.

James Bond and the Type 1 Diabetic Bridesmaid

What would Q think?
This is the time
before pens, when bottles
were the order of the day,
when syringes were sealed like fish
in their plastic sleeves.

This is the time
post-*License to Kill,* pre-*Golden Eye*
where one of six bridesmaids
has much to learn
about Fendi sling-backs, the need
to conceal, and things Episcopalian.

This is the scene beforehand:
A Hilton bedspread,
glucose tablets pinched in florist wire
for roses and Monte Cassinos
in tomorrow's bouquet,
a Medic-Alert bracelet slung
beside garters for
under-the-table injections.

She's ruled some things out:
the knife holder from Chinatown
now unsnapped from her thigh,
jellybeans hand-sewn to bra straps,
elastic candy wristlets
to bite at the slightest low.

This is the time
to be homesick for *Q*, his practicality,
his knowledge of her weak spots,

and his tricks
for all of life outside the lab.
She rarely has to lie.

No rooftop chase through Istanbul, this
is undercover all the same.
And it's increments further
than a throaty "trust no one, James."
She cannot trust her own body.

This is the film's end,
the freeing of sharks
and polishing of cars, the pause.
This is her yearning
for that impossible switch
to auto-pilot.

Little Prophets

In Germany they mean dessert:
kleine Propheten
spoons placed above dinner plates.

No lyre-playing. No smoke,
no men backing
away from The Voice
in dreamy, Old Testament surprise
fingering beards, balancing
on the balls of their feet
like tennis players at the net.

These spoons
prophesize, promise, wield
Pavlovian signals.
Their presence guarantees more
an uncomplicated more,
and tonight,
at least, it will be good.

"I am Ready to go Home"

Women's restroom graffiti, Bohemia Bagel, Prague

No politics, no jokes
no reference to Danny / Ivan / Andy's stamina.
Just home. Just the being ready.

From a stall-door guest book
this side of the Vltava
I envy Dorothy her Kansas and you—
                 with your pen—
your still-sharp point of return.
Who else paused
when snapping back the lock?
Who else re-entered
these streets of jaded charm with *yes*
in their teeth?

I would snatch your ruby slippers.
I would slit Toto's throat
and have words with witches
if it brought back home
if it brought back me,
my pushpin body
                 hard, colorful,
marking any map with purpose.

Trying to Write Nature

I.

Walking the Appalachian Trail
I stop to eat potato chips
and dangle my legs from a footbridge.
I should unwrap bread from linen—
the nutty, heavy kind—
while tonguing the pit
of a nectarine. I should know the names
of that tree, of that bird.
I should be through-hiking for weeks,
not traipsing for hours.

But everything in nature
reminds me of something man-made.
Even now, I bet tonight's sky
will be the color of cough syrup,
a tint of paint, a childhood bikini.

The air on my throat reminds me
of the air on a steel balcony, traffic
surging beneath my feet,
ambulance sirens, French horn practice
in the flat upstairs.

II.

On our backs in yoga-darkness
when meditation starts
we're to *picture a field,*
picture *lying near a stream,* not Lycra-clad
on a polished floor.
But I know the reality of fields

of thistles, rain, rocks, cow shit.
And so I imagine a couch,
an alternative where I lie with books
in lamp-lit quiet.
My breathing eases.
I am grateful for creation indirectly,
which is also fine.

II. What Every Battle Has

One Icon Speaks

Acrylic and gold leaf on a Masonite clip board

Mary with her legs crossed speaks.
Gabriel's arm and wing just visible,
Mary with her long cheeks and raised hands
mouths *choice* in thirty languages.

Gabriel's arm and wing just visible
she leans in, looks straight,
mouths *choice* in thirty languages
because she was given one.

She leans in, looks straight.
Bodies are easy to come by. Bodies are everywhere
because she was given one.
God forced nothing. God asked.

Bodies are easy to come by. Bodies are everywhere.
A womb is a room she explains.
God forced nothing. God asked.
Without choice I'm an animal, a field, a reef.

A womb is a room she explains,
I own the key to mine.
Without choice I'm an animal, a field, a reef.
Girls aren't here to bully and deride.

I own the key to mine.
Mary, with her long cheeks and raised hands—
Girls aren't here to bully and deride—
Mary with her legs crossed speaks.

Replica

From the living room carpet
tractors poke up the ramp
toward the doll-sized hay mow.
This barn's scars
come from plastic roosters,
toddler's teeth, weight bearing down
on the plywood spine.
These reflexes are no accident.
The intention is to let
small eyes, thumbs, fingers
understand
the path things take
when pulled by other things.

Built to scale and AM radio
in a starter-house garage,
three coats of varnish stroked
across a gambrel roof
and he had it done by Christmas.

One tornado-backhand
stilled *that* barn, that farm's heart—
raked off its foundation.

To rebuild is not to build again.
To rebuild is to want to build again.
Flip open the doors.
See? Like any ghost,
you can run your hand
right through it.

Flying low Over Chester County, Pennsylvania at Night

The sky's on its back.
Highways pump veins of light
toward Philadelphia.
Ice rattles in the plastic cup.
I want Thomas Eakins
in the next seat, seeing
the organs of the land,
the made earth,
muscle-real and named.
I want Eakins in the next seat, seeing
the Schuylkill opened up,
its rushing tendons still familiar
from this high.

Draw what you see,
not what you think you see.
Remember
knives slotted in their case like oars,
the scalpel in Dr. Gross's hand,
carmine-wet and warm.

Steal nature's tools
from all points of view: drying biceps
to river's mouths to anatomy
from up here, this land lit
and stretching.

Know what you see is incomplete.
I want Eakins in the next seat.

Pretending to be Italian

Ignore the snow,
the radio singing basketball scores,
this entire block
of shutters that don't close
and were never meant to.
Fill your fists
with the volcano of flour and egg
on the worktop
of your non-Italian kitchen.

Think the instant espresso
in your Wisconsin-is-for-Lovers mug
is fresh from the bar
in the village square,
proffered by the aunt of a Palio jockey.

In the museum calendar
St. Anne just gave birth to Mary.

Leaning from the bed,
Anne's gray-faced Venus-of-the-moment
ignites the planned air.
In the hot precision
of Lorenzetti's foreshadowing
she's pretending
to be someone else, too.

First Day of the Battle

Punching her apron with her knees
Harriet walked, wished.
Where an instant before
there had been fields
and woods and the peacefulness
of the Sabbath day . . .
the earth grew soldiers by the thousands.
She pivot-turned to sprint for the barn,
for her dead daughter's mare
that last, live piece of her—
racing the gauntlet of *Madam!*
Where are the Yankees?
How many are out there, Madam?
her elbows digging the air
like scythes through each *Where?*
Where are the Yankees?

Every battle has a first day,
a first woman, with uncanny timing
and something to lose
and something freshly lost.
When Harriet's moment came,
when the day cracked open
and she wanted only a tent flap in time
to disappear through,
her apron a sail, her Gettysburg
a door in the ground wherefrom
they rose, she'd later say as *if by magic—*

After Margaret S. Creighton's *The Colors of Courage: Gettysburg's Forgotten History: Immigrants, Women, and African Americans in the Civil War's Defining Battle.* Harriet Bayly was one of the first residents to see troops approaching the town.

Green Card Prayer on the Turnpike

The backseat cradles proof:
papers, records, all of it
reaching backwards
to the firm hand of the Diaconess
yanking him into this world.
   We practice in English
in ironed shirts, look
straight ahead, not listening
to the radio, not drinking
the travel mug coffee.
   We practice. He prays
not to forget
the color of my toothbrush,
our last anniversary,
which bank account
was opened in which month,
in which decade.
   We practice. I know
this man; I might fail to prove it.
In the lull of our familiar
we turn to God and the fog
hurling eastward this ordinary,
not at all ordinary day.
   We practice. We pray.

Song for Type 1 Diabetes

Could be blues,
harmonica lip-crushings,
a healthy body walking out,
cells pivot-turning
with chins in the air—an inside job,
a hard-luck soft-sell,
and it isn't going very well.
Hard times
don't always look hard,
and blue is blood's true color
before it hits air.

Could be a campfire round
sung below
an orange heel of moon,
beside the cabin, above the dock—
a harmony of luck, on and on
between the bright bellies
of lanterns, and what
could be more chronic?

Metal, possibly, and heavy,
drumstick-snapping, bass-hurling,
knees on the stage,
wet-necked wail—
the thousand-sticking screams,
not pain, but repetition, just.

>

Could be a jump-rope-rhyme
hand-heels churning air,
bangs in the eyes,
a chant from memory, from habit,
the staccato double-dutch slap
of rope on sidewalk.

Could never be a lullaby.

It's a psalm, after all.
That's no small thing.

Blessed be the test-strip vials,
O my soul
the cartridges, each ultra-fine fang,
the experimental pig
and ornaments of history
on insulin's family tree.
O my soul.
Blessed be—

Another Ex-Expatriate

I live my life in widening rings
which spread over earth and sky.
I may not ever complete the last one,
but that is what I will try.
– Rainer Maria Rilke

I live my life in widening rings
caught by a tug umbilical that brings
its welcome-backs in hula hoops of sound
invisible, from hip to ground—
reaching for unreachable things.
I live my life in widening rings

which spread over earth and sky
pierced by airplane landings. Goodbye
is what I say each morning
to the country of my adulthood. A warning
against future hellos and links I forever untie
which spread over earth and sky.

I may not ever complete the last one,
the final split. But I'm done
chasing this untethering, this fresh remorse
westward-bound without a horse
and a future roping ovals at the sun.
I may not ever complete the last one

but that is what I will try—
an emigrant back with a prodigal sigh
and half a heart across the sea,
a part-person unable to be free,
found, finally, no longer my own self's spy,
but that is what I will try.

Taxidermy in South Central Pennsylvania

I.

It's a roadside faux-Bavarian restaurant
with decent beer, fat gravy,
postcards from Munich and Oberammergau
shingled above its cash register.
Here starts the parade of heads
mounted in intervals
like past presidents
or kindergarten alphabets
in wood and brass, hairy things of all sizes:
deer to squirrels, to small
creatures of uncertain origin.
It's the turkey, though,
at the far end of the dining room,
harpooned behind the bear
onto the knotty paneling,
the turkey that keeps me looking up
from the table, the entire bird, head high,
legs splayed, asking
with every rotation of our jaws:
How did I get here?

II.

Army canteens, wool rugs,
ladles old enough to have dipped soup
for Gustav Adolf himself
line the backyard sauna.
From his pine-planked shoulders
a caribou presides
over these shared meters
of recreated Sweden.
I stand released from the vice of heat.
I inhale, my ribs slick
and heaving, brows knit in half-pain
at my searing earring posts.
In lantern-light his eyes of glass sparkle,
his nostrils flex. We are someplace
other than this place.
I would answer any question he asked,
my pelted priest.
I haven't felt this unalone in years.

III.

A second-hand store in Carlisle
is not the worst place
for a thirty-year-old, three-point buck
with a lovely neck to land.
It beats the laundry basket
in Colonel Shearling's garage.
He'd like a room with rocking chairs,
with whisky decanters
and *Playboys* from the 60's
stacked between *Life* and
North American Whitetail. He'd like
to be near Tuscarora again.
Mainly, he wants to avoid
being driven across state lines
in a rented Lexus and hung
in a flat with chandeliers,
brass doorknobs and a cat. A cat.
He can face anything
but a weekend antiquer
with scopes for eyes.

Kitchen Meditation on the 22ⁿᵈ Article of the Augsburg Confession

Not just the bread
the wine, too—the full deal.
        [hardly revolutionary now]

Behind the whisk
of batter, whack of eggs
splash of milk, stain of grape juice
financial austerity on the radio
pop-hackle-sing of hot oil
snow falling faster and faster outside
I'm thinking: bread, wine, access.
        [hardly revolutionary now]

I'm thinking of the year 1530, and I
am still the Pöbel, the rabble, the 99%.
But this document said *yes*
said *both*. I hear yes
in the kettle-keen, in the citrus sting
and every sharp blessing
I taste and take for granted.
        [still revolutionary now]

Itasca

Headwaters of the Mississippi

Splinging-cold and ready—
before it gathers speed
tugging at the zipper
this is The River on training wheels

before it gathers speed
(this makes the rest possible)
this is The River on training wheels
just watch.

This makes the rest possible.
Oh prodigal-in-the-making
just watch
the diving board flexes; the foal stands.

Oh prodigal-in-the-making,
Minnesota-minted
the diving board flexes; the foal stands.
A novice can surprise you.

Minnesota-minted
tugging at the zipper
a novice can surprise you, especially
one splinging-cold and ready.

Circus Girls at the new Pastor's Installation

Stopped to winter here,
they're seeking gigs.
The new pastor said *come join us.*
Come. Today fingers
seize cup handles, crease napkins,
push back plates, clear the stage,
the congregation
watches the sisters arrive:
boom box, long hair, leotards.

These children vault and spin,
the V's of their arms cut
another two-count silence.
Good, truly they are, but not
from circuses with names more Italian,
with larger crowds,
younger horses, and camels who
aren't always getting sick.

When the music stops
the new pastor's wife claps hard.
She claps in code
as if to say *you are good,*
don't listen to a soul tell you
your necklines
are too low, your trailers
too small. You are good,
Her hands explode,
each slap's a strike in defense
and offense.
Because she's saying to herself—
you are good. She claps knowing soon
there'll be just the pastor,

the linen tongue of the Beffchen,

a microphone cord,
a Neo-Gothic pulpit,
and plenty
of tightropes for them both.

Suddenly I Love My Hair

What weapons
it has crushed: flat irons, oils,
big-ass brushes, every
conditioner in the drug store.
This witchy frizz is not
Vogue hair, not Vanity Fair hair,
not even Woman's Day hair.

But in this waiting room,
for the first time,
we're on the same side.
This hair will exit the world before me,
nest in shower drains
and between my fingers.
This hair was not
the worst after all.

Even before the news comes
we stop being enemies.
Why does it take this long
to recognize kin?

III. The Patron Saint of T1D

Robin Hood is Gone

No hatchets, candle fat, Saracen bows.
No windchimed sunlight
fingering the leaves like hair,
bawdy, creative justice.
No whiiiiht of arrows in flight.
None of that.
Here's how the sacking is done:
                one by one by one.
Now it's paper terror,
the American NO
the daylight-dying status quo.

Personified,
a health insurance company rides
into the forest right now
with an armed escort, good weather,
the confidence of true thieves.
Hood's gang is gone.
How the sacking is done:
                trick by trick by trick.
What we're up against
is darker, stickier.

Picture wagon wheels. Picture
what's in their path.
Make way for clean kills, legal kills,
assassins at photocopiers.
A new feudalism
settles in, making normal the way
sacking is done today:
                claim by claim by claim.

Miss Hydraulic Fracturing

Here she is—
Strip Mining's half-sister
just come to our school
with sleek hair and old tricks

the homecoming queen
the girl next door
she is mascara-framed violence
walking up the main steps
she's a smile and a lie
not afraid to be new
(she has tricks up her sleeve
and tricks in her head
she has football players
in her bed
she has school board members
in her bed)

she's not her, of course,
the half-sister we know
but listen, watch
you can tell they're kin—

here we go, here we go again

The Patron Saint of T1D

Frederick Banting and Charles Best's experiments with dogs led to the discovery of insulin, one of the most significant findings in medical history.

No conversion story, no feast day,
escapes from lusty noblemen,
no tapestries or altar triptychs for her.

A disease without a proper name
doesn't get a proper saint,
just a rooftop photo
at the University of Toronto, 1921.

Type 1 diabetics owe their lives
to a martyr with no illusions: Dog 33.
Here's to Marjorie.
Here's to chasing a mystery older than Christ,
to the beta-cell enigma,
the 3,000-year conundrum.
Here's to a hot attic lab,
to uncannily willing strays and to
these stubborn, lucky men.

T1Ds have Marjorie to thank.
You don't agree? We don't mind.
Proper is a luxury.
And besides
our saint can go into the grotto
and bite your saint's ass.

Getting Back on the Horse

Lay out fears
like coyote pelts on the fence rail.
Talk about failures overcome
as if choice
is choice entirely.

At some point
you're alone with the horse.
And the devil
is in this horse, waiting
for the next round of *who's boss*.

The distance from here
to the stirrup
has nothing to do with math.
Dust etches the air these moments
where good intentions rise

from gut to gums and come
to rest in your eye
watching that horse's eye.
Not getting on
getting back on.

Red Baron Singles

Photos of pilot Manfred Albrecht Freiherr von Richthofen (The Red Baron / Der Rote Kampfflieger) were used in German WWI propaganda. Red Baron is a frozen pizza brand in the U.S.

Hunting the grid of air
above the Somme
with lethal enthusiasm,
von Richthofen made it seem
no leap at all,
that shift from horse to plane.
The sky was the new field.
Saddle to cockpit,
stirrup to stepladder,
working the stick for the Kaiser.

Cloven chin,
Tom Selleck moustache,
red scarf undulating
over slick snips of pepper,
sausage, the rug of cheese, who
is the pizza-box pilot?
Not the Ace of Aces, *wrong age,*
wrong hair, wrong everything.
Through the suction-slap
of freezer aisle doors
pizza boxes wait for shoppers,
descendants of the enemy
thinking of quick dinners, not
current wars, not
the way planes have changed
since that Albatros,
since that Fokker.

Over and over we eat the metaphor.
Hot engines, hot kitchens
publicity and fire and never
enough ways
to tell them apart.

Unpacking the Angel in South Central Pennsylvania

After Gillian Clarke

      You'll recognize an ex-expatriate Christmas angel
by one eyebrow slightly cocked.
Whether her forehead is enamel, porcelain,
pine or a batting-stuffed sock,
it'll be there—this arc. Both jaded and relaxed
she knows coming home's
a thing of heaven, not earth, a moving target.

      Beneath her toes: the scatter
of Erzgebirge mangers, traveling brush salesmen,
Hawaiian lambs glued from nuts,
candles mashed in their tin clips,
whip of electric lights,
the usual suspects in glass, dough, metal,
handled by fingers flush in disappointment,
in happiness or fatigue depending
on the continent, depending on the December.

      The angel presides uncritically.
In the dark, just the tree turned on,
smudges of light blur the branches, the room,
the town, leaving mere suggestions
of ornaments, of futures unlived,
badges earned, tokens saved—
all water under the dry bridge of her wings.

Obelisks

See them falling from the sky
like lean men in a Magritte painting.
Egypt's obelisks have landed
right-side-up and smiling
from Place de la Concorde
to Central Park.
Their ghosts also appear
as granite offspring imitations.
You'll find them
on the graves of grandparents
flanking cemetery
and mausoleum entrances in towns
where no one talks
of Karnak, of Tell el Amarna,
or the Goddess Nut.

Pried from the desert floor
the obelisks were topped
with gleaming hats,
metallic mirrors to catch
the sun's energy and anger.
Tattooed with praise
for pharaohs well-preserved
in death and memory.

Everybody loves an obelisk.
Mysteriously familiar
as churchless spires
and treasure maps combined
they resemble beautiful,
yet extremely old actresses
who haven't lost
their posture or their knack

for knowing which secrets to reveal.
They have seen better times.
The once-proud guards
of temple forecourts dragged far
from their hot homes
to the parks of foreign cities
where kites and pigeons
choke the view.

Their portraits appear
in coffee table books,
on spot-varnished pages with plenty
of white space combing the text.
On display they are,
for everyone's purposes
but their own.

Still, an obelisk is always
on speaking terms with eternity.
And even London's fist of fog
cannot hide all the sharpness
of Cleopatra's Needle.

Oregon

Next door the cowboys cinch down
the girth of their barrel-bull,

clamp thighs to its rusting belly,
slide a gloved hand forward

each in turn, and hold on for all
they're worth and more

as the others jerk, pull, shout, swing
from the chains, focused on the ride

a real bull will give them.
A real bull will not be kind.

The whole scene's a cockeyed blur
as each boy's slung

onto the old mattress, then rolling
in the dirt to stand casually and spit:

a fierce dart of tobacco. An answer.
Saliva transformed, here,

where Wranglers pack round buckles,
square asses, the hard wheels

of Copenhagen cans. A display
perfect for practice, the language

of spitting cuts through
what words can't handle anyway.

The Accidental German

Now she shakes
lots of hands, drinks coffee
from matching cups and saucers,
recites the Lord's Prayer
in German,
measures in centimeters
and grams. She listens to questions
about her former home:

> *Why are there so many guns?*
> *So many hamburgers?*

She refuses to scrub her windows
and front steps
until they're clean enough
to lick (a sin).
She lights candles at every meal,
says good morning,
good evening, good day.

> *Why are there so many fat people?*
> *So many skyscrapers?*

She boards the train each morning
with her crumbling briefcase,
watches the Rhine
muscle its way through the vineyards,
gets sentimental
for Methodist Churches, rodeo queens
and motel ice machines.

> *Why are Americans so shallow?*
> *So friendly?*

The Accidental German
watches church spires
of her current horizon
needle their way into the fog.
She's a breathing souvenir here,

someone's piece
of American apple pie
brought back to the Fatherland
for flavoring.
Back to the Fatherland
for spice.

Marlboro Country Remembered

Movie theater advertisement, Frankfurt am Main, Germany

At the movies we sit clutching open beers
and sweet popcorn, stunned
by mountain profiles.
Out there it's all campfires and rope tricks.
Space like that can make you dizzy
when your own horizon stops
at the concrete torso
of the building next door.

Like the steely shove
of a barn door my West rolls back
to the rodeo mamma next door:
homemade jeans, sunglasses raked
into her black roots—
a glass of wine in one hand,
a whip in the other.
My West comes back with the thwuhtt of spit
by the stock tank
and dogs trained to worry
steers' heels on signal.

Then my head was packed
with big ideas—
thoughts wide as Paul Bunyan's arm span.
Now they're pigeonholed
to fit, and rusty
as the language I once spoke.

But here I am smoldering.
Here I am, lit.

Christmas Eve, Feeding the Bull Calves

       Afterward
their marble-cake faces shrug
side-to-side in collars
of braided twine.
The laundry tub receives
its armload-crash of bottles
and the scalding rush
of water before saliva dries
in the nipples and a little soap
still goes a long way.
       Afterward,
this barn could be any barn,
a shell of metal, wood,
stone, mud, hide, air,
the barn.
What is it about a cow
as witness? The warm anchor
of a bovine body, the tea cup temples?
These fellows
are pre-steer.
       Afterward,
a few months on,
they'll get their introduction,
their pasture tour,
spring's first razored-lick of fence
and—most startling—
all that sky.
But now the force is here.
Now their tongues
are the center of the earth.

Reisekapellen

Tiny chapels of stone or brick
built in gratitude so overpowering
it needed the act of building
and had the funds to make it happen:
"travel chapels" because
in those days, someone of means arrived
at his destination
despite wolves, robber knights,
bears, crappy roads,
crappy carriage wheels, rain,
and no-joking pre-electricity darkness.

At my office, in this century,
I hang up the phone
with such gratitude. This time,
the lab results bring no news
(which is good news).
I draw the outline of what looks
like a shed with a steeple,
pin the sketch above my desk:
a chapel icon
for all journeys, every split second,
on water and land, someone
out there is underway.
From point B
to point A, someone
is just ahead of the wolves,
quick fingers, stolen swords
hell-weather, chance.

Today I've arrived safely.
Here's my Reisekapelle reminder,

my graphite thank you.
I'll be traveling again,
as will you. Let us be mindful.

The Boxer's Dog

The boxer's Irish Wolfhound
palms a basketball across hardwood,
basks in our mirrored glances,
eats like a giant goat.
Wine corks, doll's hands, ibuprofen,
entire towels have gone through him.
He lopes past Sharkey's photo
and the speed bags,
toward Ali and the line
of Cuban newsprint shoulders.

Hematite eyes and surfer-hair
charm us blind until
my elbow disappears inside his mouth
with delicate, peach-picking speed.

The air crackles. Just a reminder.
His ancestors could
drag soldiers from their horses,
trained forces in the fog.
Then he's gentle again, and grinning.
Mascot, brother, myth
he knows the stance: remain
about to spring, but only about to.

IV. WELCOME. COME ON DOWN.

"Lord, in Your Mercedes, Hear our Prayer"

It starts that young:
mishearing mercy.
In bed, a child prays with her mother
and a chorus line of animals
backed against the headboard.

The liturgy's familiar as the organ
with its bottom row of pipes
sticking straight out like shot guns
between the choir.
She keeps her eye on them.

And tonight, where we are,
who's to say where the Lord is, exactly?

Worse things can be dreamed
than a shepherd in a CLK 500 coupe,
a backseat full of lambs,
and a jug of juice looking like wine
(she's on to this already)
hot on the trail of that one
who wanders off again, and again.

Thirteen Ways of Looking at a Lancet

From pockets and purse floors
of T1Ds they collect
like spare change, like bobby pins.

Mountains of them bloom
in the wake of a finger-sticking life,
could fill eight jam jars a year.

A scalpel for Dr. Barbie
in long-legged scrubs
and penny-sized mask.

Thrust at thumb and finger-cheeks,
like the cuckoo bill,
through his tiny clock shutters.

200 wait in the slick paper skin
of each box: sterile
sterili steriele steril steriles...

Bullet loaded in the plastic pistol,
waiting to be sprung.

Someone's fortune.

Mixed-media artwork
sandwiched in Plexiglas
and mounted on gallery walls,
the dust of blood
intentionally not boiled away.

A magnified tip in PowerPoint,
dulled exponentially per jab,
sci-fi large to teach.

Improvisation, when needed:
pinning the wings
of butterflies for display.

Find the lancet in every picture,
in a life-long Where's Waldo?

Its cap could be any cap at all,
any blue accessory.

The finger, held prone,
in the shadow
of the next lancet descending.

Girl-Moses

From what she remembers

the set-up may as well be a pheasant,
pewter jug, chrysanthemum,
gleaming table, tight pile of plumbs,
a still life, not still
beneath a million Monsoon bitch-slaps—
rain painting every surface.
   Here's a taxi locked in traffic,
   a baby in a basket.

An escort from the west coast
adoption agency carries her charge
through calf-high surges.
The street is their Nile,
its wet crush of noise a fast-tangled story
in an already tangled life.
   A baby in a basket,
   a taxi left behind in traffic.

She will get her to the airport,
to a family twelve time zones out.
The baby pouts.
A still life is control, inanimate.
She is not in control
on this Miriam-errand, but she will get her
   past every taxi locked in traffic,
   this baby, this basket.

Re-calibrating the CGM on a Bench in Kensington Gardens

Pigeons gossip and shrug.
The gadget beeps for blood.

Like London's CCTVs
the Continuous Glucose Monitor records,

a good spy in the belly fat
of a type 1 diabetic.

From a distance she could be
setting a bomb, booking

a table for brunch, tweeting
knitting, reading.

Past Weeping Beeches the slow tide
of cell phones, runners, dogs,

three-wheeled strollers flows.
What data, on any

given day, will save us,
will stop us, will give us away?

To a Hanover Potato Chip

Both china-delicate
and work-glove-rough, you
            snap, flip, shatter,
rub-crash in traffic jams of air and salt
each bubble preserved
each rick-back dive
each broken third
and cracked-off ridge.
            You are hard, fragile, ugly,
delicious—
all curves, no planes
like bodies, and
like snowflakes, there's
no other like you.
            From the earth you came
and from the kettle,
and screech-wheeled shopping cart.
For a split-second you
are loud. Spectacular. And then
your absence leaves
            a pause, an aftertaste
lonely and subtle as the end of that
kind of phone call.

Farm Road

After Andrew Wyeth: The Helga Pictures *by John Wilmerding*

There is witchcraft and hidden meaning there.
Close as thieves in a ditch we scour this field.
What's in her purse? Who braids her hair?

Its stubbled hip of hill glows warm and bare,
in their shared light. A scab of road revealed.
There is witchcraft and hidden meaning there.

The same posture is mirrored in her stare,
her spine, trees familiar enough to shield
what's in her purse. Who braids her hair?

With no sound or expectation it's air
we feel around her, air we'll never share.
There is witchcraft and hidden meaning there

and wind enough to work strands free, the fair
spill of it bound, at her slice of neck, steeled.
What's in her purse? Who braids her hair?

All the farm roads she's known, all rocking chair-
curved in their damp, weighty way concealed
there is witchcraft and hidden meaning there.
What's in her purse? Who braids her hair?

Tail Weight

Only rocks and hard places then.
"We couldn't afford toys,
so my father cut holes in my pockets"
he would say, decades later
and wink.
Depression afternoons
too much time
too little of everything else.

He built kites from trash, odd bits
all shapes and kinds,
until he made the big one,
the one needing a proper tail weight.
He and his buddy
brought out the frame
almost too big to carry.
The neighbor boy toddled by.

They tied him down screaming,
promised adventure, ran
in tandem for the launch.
The kite lifted
arced past Larson's chimney,
twine whipping from its spool
before it dawned on them
what goes up comes down.

Witnessed only by chickens
pacing a garden in figure-eights
both boys sprinted,
electricity in their saliva, fear
ramming in fork-to-filling shocks.

That it all came down in the duck pond
would stun them the rest of their lives.

One forgiving spot
in the middle of all that concrete,
sun-baked lawn, tomato cages,
rooftops, the javelins of laundry lines.
One spot.
But when does it dawn on any of us?
Too late and only
sometimes that lucky.

In the Library, Tŷ Newydd

*The National Writers' Centre for Wales, Tŷ Newydd, was the home of
British Prime Minister David Lloyd George.*

The bow of Tŷ Newydd
is this window
curving out above the beach of lawn.
Book-skinned walls exhale
the notorious two languages
and others besides.
I would say I'm sailing but
it's more muscular than that,
less the wind on its own.
A motor's somewhere, a sense
of him propelling the house.
I stand knowing
that past these trees and the Bay of Cardigan,
past the fat Atlantic
and each airplane and train it took
to get here, the van,
the motorway hike and kind lift
on the tractor
from a Penrhyn Castle gardener
all these steps—every one
and I've not travelled at all.
Just a teithiwr-on-paper.
Here in the bow, the strongest fibers
of a limb, the natural curve cut
for where a boat's
most vulnerable, I stop moving
and finally start.

The Gatekeepers

After a photo of the abandoned York Prison building from
Stephanie Gibson's series Absent Photographer

If metal calloused, if wood scabbed
        we'd be more convinced.
Each surface stretches in rich quiet
around grates, mirrors,
planks and wires in their shawls of dust.
Some are bottomless,
some daddy-long-legs-thin.
        What happened here?
The photographer knows something.
        Surfaces are her currency.
Passing through, her witness
clicks and breathes.
Surfaces imply, imply, imply—
they're gatekeepers
as much as our own faces
        (in the corner
of a once-prison
        or the gestured lug of wrinkle,
brow arch, re-moistening of lips
not quite ready to speak).

Sharps Underground Cabaret

Sharps (pl.) medical instruments with sharp points or edges that can puncture or cut skin such as scalpels, syringes, lancets, auto injectors, infusion sets, hypodermic needles, etc.

Type 1 diabetes an autoimmune disease, not the metabolic condition called type 2 diabetes.

'Course it's underground.
This disease doesn't even have a proper name.

Welcome. Come on down.
What, you ask, is a type 1 cabaret?
Think *Vanity Fair* meets the school nurse
meets Julia Child
meets Margaret Cho meets
Elvis Costello meets
an MI-5 agent at the Betty Ford Clinic meets
a kind priest.
We've got music, stand-up,
and the all-time-favorite-special-occasion-
pump-wearers' fashion show.
Where *do* you stow that pump?

Sink into the couches
behind the tables, beneath the candles.
We've got dry wine, juice shots,
impeccable acts, and people
who know type 1 from a hole in the ground.
That is the best thing,
the wildly uncommon thing:
that knowing.
Come in, come on down.
This is exclusive in a good way.
This is your bar, your cabaret.